M000038977

Really Bad Swing Thoughts

REALLY BAD
SWING THOUGHTS

PAUL FRANCIS AND PETER J. REILLY

**Andrews McMeel
Publishing**
Kansas City

Really Bad Swing Thoughts copyright © 1997 by Paul Francis and Peter J. Reilly. All rights reserved. Printed in the United States of America. No part of this book may be used or reproduced in any manner whatsoever without written permission except in the case of reprints in the context of reviews. For information, write Andrews McMeel Publishing, an Andrews McMeel Universal company, 4520 Main Street, Kansas City, Missouri 64111.

www.andrewsmcmeel.com

98 99 00 01 02 QUF 10 9 8 7 6 5 4 3 2 1

Edited by Alison Herschberg.

another idea from becker&mayer!

Library of Congress Cataloging-in-Publication Data
Reilly, Peter J., 1958–
     Really bad swing thoughts / Peter J. Reilly and Paul Francis.
       p.   cm.
     ISBN 0-8362-5190-3
     1. Golf—Humor. 2. Golf (Swing)—Humor. I. Francis, Paul
(Paul Hugo Ross) II. Title.
GV967.R36   1998
796.352'02'07—dc21   97-33471
                                                 CIP

ATTENTION: SCHOOLS AND BUSINESSES
Andrews McMeel books are available at quantity discounts with bulk purchase for educational, business, or sales promotional use. For information, please write to: Special Sales Department, Andrews McMeel Publishing, 4520 Main Street, Kansas City, Missouri 64111.

Contents

TEEING OFF

First Time with "Guaranteed Twenty Yards Longer" Driver

YOUR SWING THOUGHT:
Time to separate the men from the boys.

SOMETHING ELSE TO THINK ABOUT:
Don't scuff it—this baby cost $300.

STILL MORE THINGS TO CONSIDER:
Wait a minute . . . Twenty yards longer than what?

VISUALIZATION:
You're marching off the tee, head held high, fire in your eyes, ready for a long walk. It's a long walk back to the pro shop. And they'd better honor the money-back guarantee.

Tee Shot with Pro Watching in Group Behind

YOUR SWING THOUGHT:
Remember all twenty-five things he said and concentrate.

SOMETHING ELSE TO THINK ABOUT:
Well, if I screw up, it's his fault, right?

STILL MORE THINGS TO CONSIDER:
What's fifty dollars an hour times 785 hours?

VISUALIZATION:
How you used to drive before your first lesson.

Drive from a Highly Elevated Tee

YOUR SWING THOUGHT:
Nice and easy.

SOMETHING ELSE TO THINK ABOUT:
If there was ever a time to kill it, this is it.

STILL MORE THINGS TO CONSIDER:
I'm going to kill myself if this one doesn't fly.

VISUALIZATION:
Watching your ball in flight for what seems like hours. Suddenly you're brought back to the present when the schmuck next to you says, "You're O.B. Are you gonna hit again, or what?"

Any Shot after a Mulligan

YOUR SWING THOUGHT:
Who the heck is Mulligan anyway?

SOMETHING ELSE TO THINK ABOUT:
It's not really cheating—everyone does it.

STILL MORE THINGS TO CONSIDER:
But will I respect myself in the morning?

VISUALIZATION:
You break seventy for the first time in your life, but during the celebrations at the nineteenth, a man with horns and cloven feet appears. He points at your signed scorecard and says, "It's time for you to pay."

Par 3, 150 Yards, into the Wind, over Water

YOUR SWING THOUGHT:
This'll need a little something extra.

SOMETHING ELSE TO THINK ABOUT:
Okay. Normally this is a seven-iron, but I've got incoming wind N-NW at eight knots. I hit a little long on my last approach, but humidity is high today, the greens are soft, one extra club should do it, can't hit my six, more than a three-quarter five, maybe seven-eighths of a five, tee it up high, take dead aim. . . .

STILL MORE THINGS TO CONSIDER:
Why do *they call the wind Mariah?*

VISUALIZATION:
As the ball is sailing in the wind, bound for the plush sanctuary of green, a delicate hand reaches up from the depths, gently plucks it out of the air, and pulls it down to its watery resting place.

Teeing up after You've Hit a Hole in One

YOUR SWING THOUGHT:
This game isn't so hard.

SOMETHING ELSE TO THINK ABOUT:
If I quit now, I'll go out a star.

STILL MORE THINGS TO CONSIDER:
Hole in one. Boy, Sigmund Freud would have a field day with that.

VISUALIZATION:
After threading a needle on the first try, do it again, only this time while wearing oven mitts.

Teeing off at Pebble Beach for the First Time

YOUR SWING THOUGHT:
I am walking in the shadow of golf legends Ben Hogan, Arnold Palmer, and Jack Nicklaus.

SOMETHING ELSE TO THINK ABOUT:
What? They couldn't find a bigger water hazard than the Pacific Ocean?

STILL MORE THINGS TO CONSIDER:
Are all those people on Baywatch *drowning just so a gorgeous lifeguard will save them?*

VISUALIZATION:
Playing Carnegie Hall when you couldn't make the cut for your high school band.

Driving after a Six-Pack

YOUR SWING THOUGHT:
This Bud's for me.

SOMETHING ELSE TO THINK ABOUT:
Do two six-packs count as two items or more than ten at the express checkout?

STILL MORE THINGS TO CONSIDER:
Who told them to put a parking lot there and park cars in it anyway?

VISUALIZATION:
Trying to square dance when your legs have fallen asleep.

150-Yard Par-3 Tee Shot

YOUR SWING THOUGHT:
I smell hole in one!

SOMETHING ELSE TO THINK ABOUT:
I smell birdie!

STILL MORE THINGS TO CONSIDER:
I smell!

VISUALIZATION:
Striking out at the plate—one, two, three.

Teeing Off with an Opponent Who Insists on Shouting, "You're the Man!"

YOUR SWING THOUGHT:
Concentrate.

SOMETHING ELSE TO THINK ABOUT:
Yeah, I'm the man. You're the moron.

STILL MORE THINGS TO CONSIDER:
What's more annoying, guys who shout that or the guy who flashes the sign that says, "John 3:16"?

VISUALIZATION:
Performing brain surgery with a nurse who likes to crack her knuckles.

Teeing Off after You Called in Sick to Work

YOUR SWING THOUGHT:
Relax. Don't worry. No one's gonna find out you're playing hooky.

SOMETHING ELSE TO THINK ABOUT:
How do I explain my sunburn tomorrow?

STILL MORE THINGS TO CONSIDER:
Do golfers ever call in sick to a tournament and spend eight hours working in an office?

VISUALIZATION:
Trying to enjoy a fattening dessert when you know you've gone off your diet.

Driving Off a Par-5 Tee

YOUR SWING THOUGHT:
*Houston—we are at ten seconds and counting...
nine, eight, seven...*

SOMETHING ELSE TO THINK ABOUT:
Maybe I should use my three-wood.

STILL MORE THINGS TO CONSIDER:
*What's my score going to be on this hole, on this
round up to now, and on the entire round (best
guess) if I pull this sucker to the left and hit it out
of bounds?*

VISUALIZATION:
*You're George Foreman and you're about to deliver
the knock-out punch to some poor sucker.*

Longest-Drive Tournament

YOUR SWING THOUGHT:
Nice, smooth swing.

SOMETHING ELSE TO THINK ABOUT:
Accelerate hard at the end.

STILL MORE THINGS TO CONSIDER:
If I turn like a pretzel and really unload . . .

VISUALIZATION:
It's the following year and you are participating again—but this time at the concession stand. And no, you don't have any @#$*! pretzels.

Driving after One Beer

YOUR SWING THOUGHT:
Let the big dog eat and drink!

SOMETHING ELSE TO THINK ABOUT:
Who said you shouldn't drink and drive?

STILL MORE THINGS TO CONSIDER:
If Mickey's a mouse and Pluto's a dog, what's Goofy?

VISUALIZATION:
Trying to eat just one potato chip.

FAIRWAY SHOTS

Blind Approach Shot; Flag Hidden by Mound

YOUR SWING THOUGHT:
Visualize the flag.

SOMETHING ELSE TO THINK ABOUT:
The force is with you, Luke.

STILL MORE THINGS TO CONSIDER:
What were those things on Princess Leia's head?
Cinnamon buns?

VISUALIZATION:
Stevie Wonder playing darts against Darth Vader.

An Approach Shot You Need to Push

YOUR SWING THOUGHT:
Stick, stick, stick.

SOMETHING ELSE TO THINK ABOUT:
Should I tee up to the right or the left?

STILL MORE THINGS TO CONSIDER:
Who am I kidding? I couldn't drop the ball to the right of the pin if I was standing there.

VISUALIZATION:
Throwing a playing card into a hat from across the room.

Bump and Run Twenty Feet off the Green

YOUR SWING THOUGHT:
More control than a chip.

SOMETHING ELSE TO THINK ABOUT:
On My Three Sons, *was it Chip and Ernie or Robby and Chip who were brothers in real life?*

STILL MORE THINGS TO CONSIDER:
What was with Uncle Charlie's haircut?

VISUALIZATION:
Running with the ball in football because you're afraid to put it in the air.

From under a Low-Hanging Tree

YOUR SWING THOUGHT:
Just punch it out.

SOMETHING ELSE TO THINK ABOUT:
I oughta punch out the clown who got me up at six A.M. to play this *#@!? game!

STILL MORE THINGS TO CONSIDER:
Suddenly this club seems awfully long.

VISUALIZATION:
You're a kid with a big round head and all your little pals are pointing and laughing as you dangle, tangled up in the notorious kite-eating tree. Way to go, Charlie Brown.

Second Shot after a Perfect 280-Yard Drive

YOUR SWING THOUGHT:
What are the chances of making two great shots in a row?

SOMETHING ELSE TO THINK ABOUT:
Just don't blow this shot.

STILL MORE THINGS TO CONSIDER:
Don't blow this shot!

VISUALIZATION:
You've come up forty yards short in deep rough and you still don't know what you're going to do. Now that really blows.

Flop Shot with Untested Lob Wedge

YOUR SWING THOUGHT:
I can't miss.

SOMETHING ELSE TO THINK ABOUT:
Maybe I should have practiced with this damn thing.

STILL MORE THINGS TO CONSIDER:
How come you drive on a parkway and park on a driveway?

VISUALIZATION:
The wedge feels like a strand of spaghetti with lettuce at the end. The ball goes as far as it would if you'd hit it with a strand of spaghetti with lettuce at the end.

Shot after Your Opponent Gets an Unfair Ruling

YOUR SWING THOUGHT:
Just keep your mind on the game.

SOMETHING ELSE TO THINK ABOUT:
I could throttle the little squirt.

STILL MORE THINGS TO CONSIDER:
If I slice this enough, I think I can knock the duffer cold.

VISUALIZATION:
You're being led to the electric chair, clutching the bible you have lived by, screaming, "He had to die. It's right here in the USGA Rules of Golf!"

Ball Nestled at the Root of a Tree

YOUR SWING THOUGHT:
This club cost $125.00—swing easy.

SOMETHING ELSE TO THINK ABOUT:
If swinging was easy, I wouldn't be here.

STILL MORE THINGS TO CONSIDER:
Chunking this shot would really hurt.

VISUALIZATION:
You're Wile E. Coyote feeling the shudder go through your body after missing the roadrunner and crashing into a wall of reinforced concrete.

Hitting to the Green from Deep Rough

YOUR SWING THOUGHT:
What I need here is a weed whacker, not a five-iron.

SOMETHING ELSE TO THINK ABOUT:
What kind of fool would flub it into this jungle in the first place?

STILL MORE THINGS TO CONSIDER:
What kind of fool am I?

VISUALIZATION:
You're hacking your way through deepest, darkest Africa and come across a long-lost medical missionary. "Dr. Livingston, I presume. Don't mind me—just playing through."

Hitting out of a Divot Mark

YOUR SWING THOUGHT:
Don't try to scoop it.

SOMETHING ELSE TO THINK ABOUT:
Why didn't the last guy replace his divot?

STILL MORE THINGS TO CONSIDER:
Why do I keep asking these dumb questions?

VISUALIZATION:
Picking a sunflower seed out of the Grand Canyon with tweezers.

Fairway Shot after Being Hit with Bird Droppings

YOUR SWING THOUGHT:
Bombs away!

SOMETHING ELSE TO THINK ABOUT:
Did FDR have advance warning of Pearl Harbor?

STILL MORE THINGS TO CONSIDER:
How come you never see baby pigeons?

VISUALIZATION:
Picture the ball hitting the green like the payload of a B-52 bomber.

Second Shot after the Golfer ahead of You Has Had a Heart Attack on the Green

YOUR SWING THOUGHT:
Settle down now.

SOMETHING ELSE TO THINK ABOUT:
What a way to go!

STILL MORE THINGS TO CONSIDER:
Wonder if his widow wants to sell his clubs?

VISUALIZATION:
Follow through like the Grim Reaper swinging a scythe.

Shot through the V of a Tree

YOUR SWING THOUGHT:
Yee ha! I got me a gun sight right at the green.

SOMETHING ELSE TO THINK ABOUT:
I couldn't hit the side of a barn with a tank gun.

STILL MORE THINGS TO CONSIDER:
Trees are 80 percent air—but I'm a 20 percent golfer.

VISUALIZATION:
It's a haunted tree with a leering face, and that limb is a baseball bat poised to knock you out of the park.

Fairway Wood on Wet Grass

YOUR SWING THOUGHT:
Slippery when wet.

SOMETHING ELSE TO THINK ABOUT:
Is it steer in the direction of a skid, or skid in the direction of a steer?

STILL MORE THINGS TO CONSIDER:
If I get in a car accident on the way home, do I have on clean underwear?

VISUALIZATION:
You're center ring at the county fair, trying to grab hold of a greased pig.

Laying up on a Front-Facing Bunker

YOUR SWING THOUGHT:
Better safe than sorry.

SOMETHING ELSE TO THINK ABOUT:
Yeah, like I could even make the green.

STILL MORE THINGS TO CONSIDER:
Can you believe they wrote the entire movie
Tin Cup *around the idea of laying up or going for it?*

VISUALIZATION:
The light turns yellow, and for the first time in your life you resist putting the pedal to the metal.

Pitch Shot with Restricted Backswing

YOUR SWING THOUGHT:
Short swing—just ten P.M. to two P.M.

SOMETHING ELSE TO THINK ABOUT:
Working nine to five, what a rat race.

STILL MORE THINGS TO CONSIDER:
If 7-Elevens are open twenty-four hours, why do they have locks on the doors?

VISUALIZATION:
Parallel parking in a tight spot.

PUTTING

Practice Putt in the Office when You're Supposed to Be Working

YOUR SWING THOUGHT:
Practice makes perfect.

SOMETHING ELSE TO THINK ABOUT:
If only the greens were coated with DuPont Stainmaster™.

STILL MORE THINGS TO CONSIDER:
Is this grounds for dismissal?

VISUALIZATION:
Getting so good you can quit your job and join the tour.

Six Inches from the Cup, but Not the Green You Intended

YOUR SWING THOUGHT:
Oops!

SOMETHING ELSE TO THINK ABOUT:
As long as I'm this close . . . should I putt?

STILL MORE THINGS TO CONSIDER:
If I putt, can I take this as a score for the hole?

VISUALIZATION:
Your watch fell into a punch bowl at a ritzy party.
Just fish it out and leave before anyone notices.

Putting on Eighteen for a Score of 125

YOUR SWING THOUGHT:
Oh, boy, if I make this it will bring my handicap down to 50!

SOMETHING ELSE TO THINK ABOUT:
This wouldn't even be a good bowling score.

STILL MORE THINGS TO CONSIDER:
In Roman numerals that's CXXV.

VISUALIZATION:
Crossing the finish line in a marathon after ten hours, just to say you did it.

Putting after Too Much Coffee

YOUR SWING THOUGHT:
Make it, make it, make it, make it, make it, make it!

SOMETHING ELSE TO THINK ABOUT:
That reminds me, when I get home I need to paint the house, put in a new swimming pool, and wash the dog.

STILL MORE THINGS TO CONSIDER:
What's that loud ba-boom, ba-boom, ba-boom sound coming from my chest?

VISUALIZATION:
Trying to suppress the feeling the crew member in Alien *had before the creature burst through his abdomen.*

Putting to Win When Your Partner Is a Sore Loser with a Permit to Carry a Gun

YOUR SWING THOUGHT:
Aim dead center.

SOMETHING ELSE TO THINK ABOUT:
He wouldn't shoot me here—too many witnesses.

STILL MORE THINGS TO CONSIDER:
He knows where I live.

VISUALIZATION:
It's sunrise, you've just smoked your last cigarette, and there's a firing squad in front of you.

Up by One Stroke, Easy Putt, but You Want Your Boss to Win

YOUR SWING THOUGHT:
Miss, miss, miss!

SOMETHING ELSE TO THINK ABOUT:
It's not whether you win or lose, it's how you keep your job.

STILL MORE THINGS TO CONSIDER:
How long before unemployment kicks in?

VISUALIZATION:
Eating humble pie with a side order of crow.

Second Putt Looking at a Three-Putt

YOUR SWING THOUGHT:
You can't get there from here.

SOMETHING ELSE TO THINK ABOUT:
I need a three-iron, not a putter.

STILL MORE THINGS TO CONSIDER:
Just one degree off and the ball will be twenty feet wide by the time it gets there.

VISUALIZATION:
It's dark. Your buddies are ringing a bell by the hole while you try to hold a flashlight in your mouth to light up the target, but at least you can tell your wife this really was a seven-hour round!

BETTING

Fifty-Dollar Bet with Ten Dollars in Your Pocket

YOUR SWING THOUGHT:
Can't miss.

SOMETHING ELSE TO THINK ABOUT:
Can't afford to miss.

STILL MORE THINGS TO CONSIDER:
Just don't get the yips.

VISUALIZATION:
Yippee-ayo-kahyay. You are trying to explain to investors in a failed savings and loan that being owed a lot of money is a good thing.

Up and Down Sandy for $100

YOUR SWING THOUGHT:
I can't believe they made me show them the money.

SOMETHING ELSE TO THINK ABOUT:
At least if I scull it, there are plenty of trees to knock it onto the green.

STILL MORE THINGS TO CONSIDER:
Is it too late to bet against myself?

VISUALIZATION:
You're climbing a tree, the ball is lodged in a limb, and you can't help wondering what Arnold Palmer would do in a situation like this.

First Tee the Morning after a Drunken Bet

YOUR SWING THOUGHT:
What was that surefire swing routine I thought of last night?

SOMETHING ELSE TO THINK ABOUT:
That wasn't me talking—it was the booze.

STILL MORE THINGS TO CONSIDER:
I don't care what they say, scotch and Kahlua is not a real drink.

VISUALIZATION:
You're at a meeting. You stand up and say, "My name is John and I'm a golfaholic. I pledge I will never hit the ball again. You can bet on it."

Betting with Anniversary-Gift Money

YOUR SWING THOUGHT:
Come to papa . . . baby needs a new pair of shoes.

SOMETHING ELSE TO THINK ABOUT:
Papa will need a new place to live if he screws up.

STILL MORE THINGS TO CONSIDER:
Is there such thing as Stupid Bettors Anonymous?

VISUALIZATION:
Your wife has cleaned you out, and you're standing at a freeway on-ramp with a sign that reads, "Will Work for Green Fees."

Wearing a Kilt on a Course in Scotland on a Dare

YOUR SWING THOUGHT:
Please don't let it be windy.

SOMETHING ELSE TO THINK ABOUT:
Maybe Scotch tape was invented to hold their kilts down.

STILL MORE THINGS TO CONSIDER:
What does "Auld Lang Syne" mean anyway?

VISUALIZATION:
You've been hired to play an extra in the movie Braveheart.

Putting to Win the Hole When the Loser Has to Buy Drinks

YOUR SWING THOUGHT:
Absolut perfection.

SOMETHING ELSE TO THINK ABOUT:
The bigger the beer belly, the bigger the bar tab.

STILL MORE THINGS TO CONSIDER:
I'll need a home equity loan to keep these guys in beers.

VISUALIZATION:
You have to drop an olive in a martini glass—from twenty feet.

Buddy Bets You Ten Bucks You Can't Make It in Long Carry over Water

YOUR SWING THOUGHT:
Money in the bank.

SOMETHING ELSE TO THINK ABOUT:
Would you like that in two fives or ten singles?

STILL MORE THINGS TO CONSIDER:
If I add in the price of the ball I'll be down $11.50.

VISUALIZATION:
Crossing the Atlantic on the Titanic.

OOPS!

First Shot Feeling Effects of Last Night's Chili

YOUR SWING THOUGHT:
I hope I'm downwind.

SOMETHING ELSE TO THINK ABOUT:
Act calm and maybe the guys won't notice.

STILL MORE THINGS TO CONSIDER:
If I swing too hard all hell will break loose.

VISUALIZATION:
Your club digs into the tee, which is made of steaming beans and a fiery red sauce, and the fall-out covers your buddies. Oops—chili-dipped it!

Second Shot from a
Crowded Driving Range

YOUR SWING THOUGHT:
*Quick, hit it and get outta here before anyone
sees me.*

SOMETHING ELSE TO THINK ABOUT:
Hey—I think they're aiming right for me!

STILL MORE THINGS TO CONSIDER:
Can golf balls kill?

VISUALIZATION:
Mr. Sulu, activate the shields!

Any Shot When Your Son Is about to Beat You for the First Time

YOUR SWING THOUGHT:
He's a chip off the old block.

SOMETHING ELSE TO THINK ABOUT:
If he chips this in, I'll knock his block off.

STILL MORE THINGS TO CONSIDER:
He must get his competitiveness from his mother.

VISUALIZATION:
It's a scene from The Godfather. *"Son, you're the golfer in the family now. I'm just going to spend my remaining days chipping and putting in the backyard from now on. But if you ever need advice, say, about playing around trees, I've got the experience."*

Any Shot after Smashing a Car Windshield in the Parking Lot

YOUR SWING THOUGHT:
Like that hasn't happened to every golfer.

SOMETHING ELSE TO THINK ABOUT:
They'll never know it was me—you can't get there from here.

STILL MORE THINGS TO CONSIDER:
I don't like the way everyone's pointing at me.

VISUALIZATION:
A very large man is explaining the pain involved, depending where he decides to put his Big Bertha, as he rifles through your wallet.

Shot after You've Hit into the Group ahead of You

YOUR SWING THOUGHT:
It's not my day.

SOMETHING ELSE TO THINK ABOUT:
That very large man looks familiar.

STILL MORE THINGS TO CONSIDER:
I don't like the way everyone's pointing at me.

VISUALIZATION:
No more explanation needed about the pain involved from a well-placed Big Bertha.

Hitting a Shot Left-Handed

YOUR SWING THOUGHT:
It'd be easier to put my elbow in my ear.

SOMETHING ELSE TO THINK ABOUT:
I never appreciated how talented Mickelson really is.

STILL MORE THINGS TO CONSIDER:
Then again, if he can do it, it can't be that difficult.

VISUALIZATION:
Your friends are looking down at you, flat on your back, frantically trying to extricate your elbow from your ear.

From a Neighboring Home's Patio

YOUR SWING THOUGHT:
Be careful not to scrape your club on the concrete.

SOMETHING ELSE TO THINK ABOUT:
It's their own fault for building so close to the fairway.

STILL MORE THINGS TO CONSIDER:
Is that the sound of a barking Doberman getting closer?

VISUALIZATION:
An enemy grenade has just landed in your barracks window—toss it back and then run for cover.

Any Shot with Hiccups

YOUR SWING THOUGHT:
Hurry up and swing before the next . . .

SOMETHING ELSE TO THINK ABOUT:
"Hiccup" sounds like it is; so does "cough." Why isn't the word for sneeze "ahchoo"?

STILL MORE THINGS TO CONSIDER:
Aren't hiccups one of the first symptoms of ebola?

VISUALIZATION:
Trying not to spill your coffee while driving over potholes.

Next Shot after Your Ball Lands in the Back of a Passing Cart

YOUR SWING THOUGHT:
Don't let that throw you.

SOMETHING ELSE TO THINK ABOUT:
Add in the distance the cart traveled and that's my longest drive ever.

STILL MORE THINGS TO CONSIDER:
How come I can hit a moving target, but not the green, which is still?

VISUALIZATION:
Think of hitting the green as target practice versus skeet shooting.

A Full Bladder, Five Holes from the Nearest Rest Room

YOUR SWING THOUGHT:
A nice fluid motion . . . I mean, no cancel that thought!

SOMETHING ELSE TO THINK ABOUT:
Now this is what I call a water hazard.

STILL MORE THINGS TO CONSIDER:
I wonder what June Allyson makes for those Depends commercials.

VISUALIZATION:
The little Dutch boy with his finger in the dike.

Any Shot after Your Ball Is Swallowed by an Alligator

YOUR SWING THOUGHT:
See ya later, alligator!

SOMETHING ELSE TO THINK ABOUT:
Does anybody really like the taste of Gatorade?

STILL MORE THINGS TO CONSIDER:
Better golfer—Godzilla or Mothra?

VISUALIZATION:
Playing a round on a golf course in Jurassic Park.

An Iron Shot after Lightning Strikes a Nearby Tree

YOUR SWING THOUGHT:
I've got a bag with eleven lightning rods in it!

SOMETHING ELSE TO THINK ABOUT:
Who says lightning never strikes twice?

STILL MORE THINGS TO CONSIDER:
Am I paid up on my life insurance premium?

VISUALIZATION:
Playing soccer in a minefield.

Any Shot after Scarfing Down a Chili Dog on the Turn

YOUR SWING THOUGHT:
Let 'er rip!

SOMETHING ELSE TO THINK ABOUT:
Did anyone hear that?

STILL MORE THINGS TO CONSIDER:
If it's all beef, why isn't it called hot bull?

VISUALIZATION:
The campfire scene in Mel Brooks's Blazing Saddles.

Any Shot When You've Sneaked onto an Exclusive Course

YOUR SWING THOUGHT:
Look natural.

SOMETHING ELSE TO THINK ABOUT:
Fifty bucks I've saved!

STILL MORE THINGS TO CONSIDER:
Is a trespassing fine more than fifty bucks?

VISUALIZATION:
Crashing a black-tie wedding gala dressed in jeans.

Any Shot with Allergies During Ragweed Season

YOUR SWING THOUGHT:
Don't sneeze . . . ahhhh, ahhhh, ahhhh . . . shoot!

SOMETHING ELSE TO THINK ABOUT:
Why "hay fever"? It's not hay and there's no fever.

STILL MORE THINGS TO CONSIDER:
Shouldn't a handkerchief be called a nosekerchief?

VISUALIZATION:
Trying not to laugh when you're being tickled with a feather duster.

Shot after Removing the Ball from the Cart Path

YOUR SWING THOUGHT:
Stay on the grass.

SOMETHING ELSE TO THINK ABOUT:
But I did get a good bounce.

STILL MORE THINGS TO CONSIDER:
If fairways were asphalt, everyone would eagle on par 5s.

VISUALIZATION:
Playing baseball with a Super Ball.

Any Shot with a Blister on Your Hand

YOUR SWING THOUGHT:
Stay loose and block out the pain.

SOMETHING ELSE TO THINK ABOUT:
How does an aspirin find your sore spot?

STILL MORE THINGS TO CONSIDER:
If they wanted Band-Aids to be flesh color, why not make them clear plastic from the beginning?

VISUALIZATION:
Running a marathon with a rock in your shoe.

OPPOSITE SEX

Tee Shot, Teamed up with a Beautiful Woman

YOUR SWING THOUGHT:
Glad I didn't have the chili last night!

SOMETHING ELSE TO THINK ABOUT:
Sex.

STILL MORE THINGS TO CONSIDER:
Did I remember to brush my teeth?

VISUALIZATION:
You're playing Pebble Beach with her. She's naked.

First Shot Teamed up with a Handsome Hunk

YOUR SWING THOUGHT:
Hope I don't have spinach in my teeth.

SOMETHING ELSE TO THINK ABOUT:
Romance.

STILL MORE THINGS TO CONSIDER:
Did I remember to use roll-on?

VISUALIZATION:
You're lying on a pebbly beach, his heaving chest glistens from the heat of passion.

Playing with Your Mother-in-Law

YOUR SWING THOUGHT:
Show no mercy!

SOMETHING ELSE TO THINK ABOUT:
Mercy, what am I thinking? She always beats me.

STILL MORE THINGS TO CONSIDER:
I shouldn't be that competitive with a sweet little old lady.

VISUALIZATION:
She has a 35-footer to win at the eighteenth and says, "If I make this, I'll just die." You can't help it and say, "That's a gimmee!"

Playing in a Husband/Wife Tournament

YOUR SWING THOUGHT:
Now we'll find out if any golf day is a good day.

SOMETHING ELSE TO THINK ABOUT:
How come this hole is sponsored by a divorce lawyer?

STILL MORE THINGS TO CONSIDER:
Time to show the little lady who's king of this course.

VISUALIZATION:
You're pushed to the back of a cheering crowd that holds aloft the new course record holder. Your wife is looking down at you apologetically.

Opening Drive on First Round Ever with Wife

YOUR SWING THOUGHT:
Now she'll know it doesn't take seven hours to play a round.

SOMETHING ELSE TO THINK ABOUT:
I hope she doesn't think this means I've been playing around.

STILL MORE THINGS TO CONSIDER:
Didn't that guy in the clubhouse say he was a divorce lawyer—what was his name?

VISUALIZATION:
You're leaving divorce court with all your worldly possessions you've been allowed to keep: a putter and a bag of old balls.

Teeing Off in a Pro-Am with Female Pro

YOUR SWING THOUGHT:
No woman's gonna out-drive me.

SOMETHING ELSE TO THINK ABOUT:
If I don't make the ladies' tee, do I have to wait for her tee shot before I hit again?

STILL MORE THINGS TO CONSIDER:
She's pretty cute . . . I hope I'm not wearing those "World's Best Dad" boxer shorts.

VISUALIZATION:
You're making that embarrassing walk to the green and it's worse than you feared—you realize you're wearing those lucky, hole-riddled jockeys.

Teamed in a Coed Tourney with a Transsexual

YOUR SWING THOUGHT:
Keep your eye on the balls, er . . . ball.

SOMETHING ELSE TO THINK ABOUT:
Grandma, what big hands you have.

STILL MORE THINGS TO CONSIDER:
That's a lot to go through just to hit from the ladies' tee.

VISUALIZATION:
Racing the old East German swim team in the 200-meter freestyle.

TOURNAMENT
PLAY

Million-Dollar Hole in One

YOUR SWING THOUGHT:
Wonder what the odds are?

SOMETHING ELSE TO THINK ABOUT:
Should I invest the money in munis or junk bonds?

STILL MORE THINGS TO CONSIDER:
I can see it now: limos, money—a winner at last!

VISUALIZATION:
You're driving your '85 Hyundai home, explaining to the kids that money can't buy happiness and it's not the winning it's the playing, as a fleet of limos passes you by.

Driving on Par 3 in a Tournament in Which a Hole in One Wins a Car

YOUR SWING THOUGHT:
Park this baby in the garage.

SOMETHING ELSE TO THINK ABOUT:
Will my clubs fit in the trunk?

STILL MORE THINGS TO CONSIDER:
Why do the British use sissy names like lorry *for* truck *and* bonnet *for the car hood?*

VISUALIZATION:
Trying to find your car in the parking lot at Disney World. On Saturday.

Starting the Back Nine When You're the Worst Player in a Tournament Foursome

YOUR SWING THOUGHT:
Stay positive.

SOMETHING ELSE TO THINK ABOUT:
You can still turn it around.

STILL MORE THINGS TO CONSIDER:
I can pretend to sprain my ankle and beg out.

VISUALIZATION:
Heading downhill fast with no brakes.

Club Tournament; You Lied about Your Handicap

YOUR SWING THOUGHT:
Honesty really would have been the best policy.

SOMETHING ELSE TO THINK ABOUT:
All I need is my best round ever.

STILL MORE THINGS TO CONSIDER:
I think I peaked five years ago.

VISUALIZATION:
You're a naked emperor striding through a jeering throng.

TRAPS

Caught in a Tree Branch

YOUR SWING THOUGHT:
What would Arnold Palmer do in a situation like this?

SOMETHING ELSE TO THINK ABOUT:
What am I saying? Arnold Palmer wouldn't be in this situation.

STILL MORE THINGS TO CONSIDER:
Sometimes in golf you just gotta go out on a limb.

VISUALIZATION:
You're walking a tightrope, 100 feet in the air, with a fully loaded golf bag to keep you balanced.

Downhill Putt toward Water

YOUR SWING THOUGHT:
Maybe I should have bought those floating balls after all.

SOMETHING ELSE TO THINK ABOUT:
At least it's just a lake ball.

STILL MORE THINGS TO CONSIDER:
Hope it doesn't feel homesick.

VISUALIZATION:
You're trying to roll a marble along the dining table, making it stop dead on the screw hole at the edge.

Fairway Bunker Shot

YOUR SWING THOUGHT:
I always choke on this shot.

SOMETHING ELSE TO THINK ABOUT:
There goes par.

STILL MORE THINGS TO CONSIDER:
What am I doing playing a course with fairway bunkers, anyway? Who do I think I'm kidding—this course is way too hard for me. Way out of my league.

VISUALIZATION:
You're in the Gulf War, in the middle of the desert, firing an 80mm howitzer at the enemy situated in a small oasis in the distance.

Hitting over Water with an Expensive Ball

YOUR SWING THOUGHT:
Fly my pretty!

SOMETHING ELSE TO THINK ABOUT:
Would this ball kill a fish if it hit one?

STILL MORE THINGS TO CONSIDER:
Maybe I'll have trout for dinner.

VISUALIZATION:
Standing over a toilet bowl flushing dollar bills.

Shot from a Deep Sand Trap with Your Ball Imbedded in Wall

YOUR SWING THOUGHT:
Explosion shot.

SOMETHING ELSE TO THINK ABOUT:
Like sand through an hourglass, so are The Days
of Our Lives.

STILL MORE THINGS TO CONSIDER:
Club sandwich and a sand wedge club. Coincidence?

VISUALIZATION:
Gregory Peck scaling a sheer rock face in The Guns
of Navarone.

Putting from a Sand Bunker

YOUR SWING THOUGHT:
Why is it called a Texas wedge?

SOMETHING ELSE TO THINK ABOUT:
Why did I forget my sand wedge?

STILL MORE THINGS TO CONSIDER:
Let's eat Italian tonight.

VISUALIZATION:
You've cracked, lying on your back making sand angels, singing the theme to Lawrence of Arabia *as your buddies putt out and move on.*

Using a Ball Retriever

YOUR SWING THOUGHT:
I've gotta get this thing regripped.

SOMETHING ELSE TO THINK ABOUT:
Wouldn't it be funny if I fell in?

STILL MORE THINGS TO CONSIDER:
I don't even like Italian.

VISUALIZATION:
I am one with the ball I am about to retrieve.

CLOSING SWING THOUGHTS

Third Shot (of Booze) at the Nineteenth Hole

YOUR SWING THOUGHT:
Head back, mouth open, nice follow-through.

SOMETHING ELSE TO THINK ABOUT:
Head back, mouth open, nice follow-through.

STILL MORE THINGS TO CONSIDER:
What's the point of sticking a tiny umbrella in a mixed drink? The inside of the glass is already wet.

VISUALIZATION:
It's seven A.M. You're clear-headed and ready for a productive day at the office. . . .

YOUR SWING THOUGHT:
Why do I put myself through this—I'm not playing again until I know what I'm doing. No golf for me next week.

SOMETHING ELSE TO THINK ABOUT:
Then again . . . the beer is cold, I love spending time with the guys on a Sunday afternoon—and what about that shot I made on number seven? . . . Even Tiger would have been proud.

STILL MORE THINGS TO CONSIDER:
There's always next week.

VISUALIZATION:
You're in the U.S. Open. It's the last day and the crowd has dubbed you John "The Phenom" Doe. Your weekend buddies are cheering along with the throng at the eighteenth as you stride to the green, mentally preparing for a three-foot putt to steal the championship away from Tiger Woods. Nothing can go wrong now—just stay calm . . . visualize . . . visualize. . . . Only a schmuck would miss this putt. . . .